HEALTH
IN THE
HUSTLE

Simple recipes for the beginner cook, time-crunched athlete, or busy adult.

Abbey Nixon

Dedications

To my mom and dad: thank you for your endless support—and for making me help in the kitchen when I was little, even when I definitely did not want to.

To my brother: I never would have finished this without your reassuring nods of approval after I asked if every single page looked okay. Your constant, highly detailed feedback is always inspiring.

To my mamaw: Thank you for showing me how food brings people together. I can't wait to give popcorn, Milk Duds, and Sun Drop to my grandchildren one day, and maybe an apple, just to balance it out.

To my roommate and best friend: thank you for eating everything I made and giving honest opinions. I promise to never make those disgusting "healthy" brownies ever again.

ABOUT THIS BOOK

Lift at 6:00 am. First class at 9, second class at 10, third class at 11. Internship from 1:00 to 3:00. Practice from 3:00 to 6:00. After practice, shower, eat, do homework, and get ready to do it all over again the next day.

That is a typical day for me as a D2 athlete; maybe this type of schedule sounds familiar to you?

When life gets busy, nutrition usually loses its spot on the priority list. If there is anything that being a college athlete has taught me, it is the importance of nutrition. Nutrition influences our mood, energy, confidence, and overall health.

During my sophomore year, I realized how much better I felt when I ate well. In addition to the challenges of a jam-packed schedule, my dorm room "kitchen" had a mini-fridge, 12 inches of counter space, and a sink that was 10 inches wide and 4 inches deep.

I wrote this book to give busy people with limited resources like me inspiration for easy and healthy meals. Whether you are a college kid on your own for the first time, an athlete who has no time or brainpower to come up with meals, or a parent looking for new ideas, I created this book with each of you in mind.

There is freedom in having the ability to fuel yourself with real food. When life gets busy, we do not have to compromise our health. I hope that this book will help you find joy in the kitchen that translates to the rest of your life!

TABLE OF CONTENTS

TABLE OF CONTENTS

EQUIPMENT

Must Haves

- oven or toaster oven/air fryer
- stovetop or hot plate
- large frying pan or electric frying pan/skillet
- knife
- cutting board
- baking sheet
- meal prep containers
- large mixing bowl

Optional Gadgets

- spatula
- lemon/lime squeezer
- oil spray bottle
- veggie chopper

TERMINOLOGY

Dice: to cut food into small, evenly sized cubes

Chop: to cut food into small, rough pieces

Saute: to cook food quickly in a small amount of oil over medium-high heat

Grease: to lightly coat a pan with oil or butter to prevent sticking

Preheat: to heat the oven or pan before adding food

Simmer: to cook liquid just below boiling, with small bubbles

Macronutrients: (macros) the three main nutrients: carbohydrates, protein, and fat

Micronutrients: vitamins and minerals needed in smaller amounts for health

Complex Carbohydrates: carbohydrates that digest slowly and provide steady energy (oats, rice, potatoes)

Lean Protein: Protein sources low in saturated fat (chicken, fish, Greek yogurt)

Meal Prep: preparing meals ahead of time to save time during the week

How to cook chicken:
1. Season both sides with salt & pepper or other seasoning blend.
2. Heat a frying pan over medium heat and add a little oil.
3. Place chicken in pan, and cook 7-10 minutes on each side.
4. Use a meat thermometer to check and see if the internal temperature has reached 165 F, or cut through the middle to make sure the chicken is no longer pink.

How to shred a rotisserie chicken:
1. Remove legs and wings.
2. Pull off breast and thigh meat from the bones.
3. Shred meat using two forks (pull apart), or use your hands for larger chunks.
4. Discard skin and bones.

How to cook ground beef or ground turkey:
1. Heat a frying pan over medium heat and add oil.
2. Add meat to the pan.
3. Break meat apart with a spatula or spoon as it cooks.
4. Cook 6-8 minutes, stirring occasionally.
5. Season once fully cooked. No pink = done.

BREAKFAST

Pancakes

Ingredients

- 2 eggs
- ½ cup milk
- 1 ½ cups oats
- 2 tsp baking powder
- 1 tsp vanilla extract
- 1/2 cup vanilla Greek yogurt
- cinnamon

Optional

- 2 bananas
- blueberries
- chocolate chips

Directions

1. Mix all ingredients together in blender until smooth.
2. Heat skillet on medium heat. Spray with oil or cover with butter. Pour small mounds from the blender onto skillet. Depending on the size of your skillet and pancakes, you may be able to fit 3-4 at a time.
3. Cook for about 1-2 min each side. You can tell they are ready to flip when sliding spatula underneath and no batter sticks to it. Lower heat to medium-low if needed.
4. Transfer pancakes to a plate, and continue cooking remaining batter. Serve with pure maple syrup, not the high fructose stuff!

Honey Banana Toast

• Makes 1 serving •

Ingredients

- 2 slices whole wheat bread or English muffin
- 2 tbsp peanut butter
- 1 banana
- drizzle of honey
- cinnamon

Directions

1. Lay out 2 slices of toast.
2. Spread peanut butter or nut butter of choice on each slice.
3. Slice 1 banana and place on toast.
4. Add a drizzle of honey and a dash of cinnamon.

Breakfast Biscuit

• Makes 8 biscuits •

Ingredients

- 8 eggs
- ½ cup cottage cheese
- English muffins
- provolone or cheddar cheese
- turkey or chicken sausage patties

Directions

1. Heat oven to 350 F. Spray 9x13 baking dish with nonstick cooking spray.
2. In a bowl, whisk together eggs. Add cottage cheese and mix. Cottage cheese is not necessary, but it adds protein. Season with salt and pepper.
3. Transfer mixture to the baking dish. Bake 25 min or until eggs have fully cooked.
4. While eggs are baking, cook sausage patties in a pan over medium heat. Flip while cooking.
5. Toast English muffins.
6. When eggs are finished baking, cut them into a circular shape to fit the biscuit. You can do this with a knife or using a plastic cup. To use a cup, hold the opening of the cup on the eggs and press down as if you are cutting a cookie shape. Save or toss leftover eggs.
7. Assemble your biscuit. Lay out the English muffins and add egg, sausage, and a slice of cheese. Before eating, place the entire biscuit in the microwave for 30-40 sec to melt cheese. Store extra biscuits in an airtight wrap or container and save for the week as a meal prep.

Sausage & Sweet Potato Hash

• Makes 4 servings •

Ingredients

- 1 package (16 oz) Italian chicken sausage
- 2 sweet potatoes
- 1 red bell pepper
- 3 cups kale

Directions

1. Preheat oven to 400 F. Dice sweet potatoes into small cubes. Prepare a sheet pan by drizzling with oil. Place diced sweet potatoes on baking sheet, drizzle oil on sweet potatoes, and bake 30 min.
2. While sweet potatoes are baking, dice bell pepper. Prepare kale by rinsing until clean, then tear the kale leaf from the center stem. Set kale aside for later use.
3. Begin heating a pan over medium heat. Cut sausage into pieces and cook in pan with the diced bell pepper. Let sausage and bell pepper cook for about 15-20 minutes, stirring occasionally.
4. When sweet potatoes finish baking, add to the pan with sausage and bell pepper. Add kale so that you have all ingredients in the pan. Let cook for about 5 minutes or until kale begins to wilt, stirring occasionally. Season with salt and pepper.

Overnight Oats

Ingredients

Base
- ½ cup oats
- ½ cup milk
- ½ cup vanilla Greek yogurt
- 1 tsp vanilla extract
- strawberries

Optional

1 tbsp chia seeds

1 tbsp pure maple syrup

1 scoop vanilla protein powder

granola

chocolate chips

Directions

1. In your preferred container (I love using mason jars), add oats, milk, and yogurt. Stir until combined.
2. Add vanilla and any other add-ins of your choosing. Stir until combined.
3. Dice strawberries, place on top of base.
4. Place in refrigerator and leave overnight.

Notes

Overnight oats are my go-to breakfast for meal prep. I can make four at a time in about 10 minutes. The combinations are endless, you can even use frozen fruit to reduce the time it takes to cut fresh fruit. If you like yours to be sweeter, just add maple syrup or additional vanilla extract.

Yogurt Bowl

• Makes 1 serving •

Ingredients

- 1 cup Greek yogurt
- ½ cup frozen raspberries
- ½ cup frozen blueberries
- ¾ cup granola
- 1 tbsp chia seeds
- honey

Directions

1. Place yogurt into a bowl.
2. Top with fruit, granola, and chia seeds.
3. Drizzle with honey.

Egg Bites

Ingredients

- 8 eggs
- ½ cup cottage cheese
- ½ cup diced bell pepper
- ½ cup freshly chopped spinach

Optional

- ¼ cup diced tomatoes
- ¼ cup shredded cheese
- ¼ cup chopped onion
- ½ diced turkey bacon or sausage

Directions

1. Heat oven to 350 F. Prepare muffin pan by spraying with nonstick cooking spray or drizzle with oil.
2. Chop bell pepper and fresh spinach and mix together in a large bowl. Using a spoon, evenly distribute the veggies into each muffin cup.
3. Next, prepare eggs. In a large bowl, crack 8 eggs and whisk together. Add cottage cheese and mix with eggs. Season with salt and pepper.
4. Carefully pour egg mixture into each muffin cup with the veggies. Fill muffin cup to about ¾ full. The eggs will rise while baking.
5. Bake for 20 minutes.

Notes

These are great for a meal prep, grab-and-go breakfast. Keep for up to five days, and reheat in the microwave or toaster oven. Pair with fruit and a slice of toast for a full meal.

LUNCH

How to Build Your Own Meal Prep

Meal prepping is a great way to prepare food and save time during the week. Having ready-to-eat meals stored in the fridge is a huge stress relief for me. It may take a little effort to put together, but it is so worth it to have in the middle of a busy day.

Each recipe in this lunch section can be meal prepped, and I also want to share how you can create your own!

The ground turkey bowl is a staple lunch for me in college. It's simple and easy to throw together. An example of how to build your own meal prep is provided below. You can mix and match any of the ingredients. Just choose your own favorite protein, carbohydrate, and veggies.

How to Build Your Own Meal Prep

Step 1: Choose base	Step 2: Choose veggies	Step 3: Choose protein
• rice • quinoa • orzo • lettuce • pasta noodles	• bell peppers • broccoli • zucchini • squash • green beans • asparagus • sweet potatoes • brussel sprouts	• ground turkey • ground beef • chicken • fish • steak • chicken sausage

Staple Combos:
- ground turkey, rice, bell peppers
- ground beef, sweet potato, broccoli
- chicken, quinoa, zucchini

Chicken Quesadillas

Ingredients

- whole grain tortillas
- 1 shredded rotisserie chicken
- low-fat shredded cheese
- 1 large bag spinach
- 1 can black beans
- salsa
- sour cream or Greek yogurt to top

Directions

1. Heat oven to 425 degrees F.
2. Shred a rotisserie chicken.
3. In a bowl, mix chicken with 1/2-1 cup salsa, a few tbsp sour cream or yogurt, salt and pepper, and beans.
4. Lay tortillas on a baking sheet. Add cheese on one half of each tortilla, lay spinach on cheese, then top with a scoop of chicken mixture.
5. Fold in half, spray or brush both sides with olive oil.
6. Bake at 425 degrees F for 10 minutes, flip, and bake another 8-10 minutes until golden and crispy.

Colorful Quinoa Mix

Ingredients

- 1 rotisserie chicken
- 2 cups quinoa
- 2 cans chickpeas
- 4 mini cucumbers
- 1 container cherry tomatoes

Dressing:
- 1/3 cup olive oil
- 1/3 cup honey
- 1 freshly squeezed lemon

Directions

1. Begin by cooking quinoa. Add 2 cups quinoa, 4 cups water to pan. Add salt or butter as desired. Turn heat to high and bring to a boil. Once boiling, reduce heat to low, cover, and simmer 15 minutes.
2. Dice cucumbers and tomatoes. Open chickpea cans and drain liquid.
3. Shred rotisserie chicken using a fork. Place in bowl.
4. To make dressing, mix together olive oil, honey and lemon by whisking together with a fork.
5. Add all ingredients together in a bowl, top with dressing.

Mediterranean Bowl

• Makes 4 servings •

Ingredients

- 8 pieces Italian chicken sausage
- 2 cups rice
- 1 package cherry tomatoes
- 6 mini cucumbers
- tzatziki sauce

Directions

1. In a medium-sized saucepan, prepare rice. Add 2 cups rice with 2 cups water, stir, and bring to a boil. Once boiling, remove from heat and cover for 15 minutes. Adding salt and butter to rice will add flavor.
2. While rice is cooking, begin heating a frying pan over medium heat. Drizzle with oil. Slice sausages and cook in frying pan 7-9 minutes.
3. Dice cherry tomatoes and cucumbers.
4. Combine all ingredients and serve with tzatziki sauce.

Notes

Tzatziki sauce can be purchased at the grocery store, but you can make your own by simply mixing plain Greek yogurt, dill, garlic powder, and salt.

Burger Bowl

Ingredients

- 1 lb lean ground beef
- ½ onion
- spring mix
- cherry tomatoes
- 2 sweet or regular potatoes
- dijon mustard

Directions

1. Heat oven to 375 F. Dice potatoes, or cut into long strips to resemble french fries. Drizzle a sheet pan with oil and place potatoes on the sheet pan. If using regular potatoes instead of sweet, season with salt and pepper. Cook in oven for 30 min. Regular potatoes take longer to cook than sweet; you will know they are done if you stick a fork in them and the potato is soft.

2. While potatoes cook, dice cherry tomatoes and chop half an onion.

3. Place a pan over medium heat. Drizzle with oil. Add chopped onion to pan, season with salt and pepper and mix with oil. Let cook for about 3 min. Add ground beef to pan with onion and cook until browned. Have fun with the seasoning! You can use paprika, chili powder, ground cumin, seasoning salt, etc.

4. Assemble bowl by adding all ingredients together. Top with mustard.

Southwestern Bowl

• Makes 4 servings •

Ingredients

- 2 chicken breasts
- 1 can corn
- 1 can black beans
- 2 cups rice
- 1 avocado
- shredded cheese to top

Directions

1. Cut chicken into bite-sized pieces. Season with salt and pepper, chili powder, and paprika. Cook in frying pan over medium heat.
2. In a saucepan, cook rice. Add 2 cups rice, 2 cups water. Bring to a boil. Once boiling, cover and let simmer 15 minutes.
3. Open can of black beans and can of corn. Pour into a single bowl and mix together. Microwave for 1-2 minutes.
4. Cut open avocado and cut into slices.
5. Assemble bowl by adding rice as the base layer, then add chicken, corn and beans, avocado, and cheese.

Simple Salad

Ingredients

- 2 chicken breasts
- 1 large bag spring mix
- 1 can chickpeas
- 4 mini cucumbers
- dried cranberries
- pecans

Dressing
- olive oil
- lemon juice
- maple syrup

Directions

1. Cut chicken into bite-sized pieces. Season well and cook on frying pan.
2. Slice cucumbers. Prepare chickpeas by first draining liquid from can, then place in a colander and rinse.
3. Assemble salad bowl. Add spring mix and top with chicken, chickpeas, cucumber slices, cranberries, and pecans.
4. For the dressing, measure with your heart. Add equal parts of each. Instead of making one big batch, you can drizzle ingredients of the dressing into each bowl. Place a lid over the meal prep bowl and shake to mix evenly.

DINNER

Bell Pepper Nachos

Ingredients

- 5 bell peppers
- 1 lb lean ground turkey
- 1 can corn
- 1 can black beans
- taco seasoning
- shredded cheese

Optional toppings:
- sour cream
- cilantro
- avocado

Directions

1. Heat the oven to 350 F
2. Cut bell peppers in half lengthwise, leaving large pieces that can be filled. Place the pepper halves cut-side up on a baking sheet. Bake in oven for 15 minutes.
3. While peppers are baking, cook ground turkey in pan. Add taco seasoning before browning. Once browned, add corn and beans. Stir.
4. When peppers are finished baking, stuff with the turkey, corn, and bean mixture. Sprinkle cheese on top.
5. Bake in oven 10 minutes.

Healthy Ramen Noodles

Ingredients

- 1 lb lean ground beef
- ¼ cup low sodium soy sauce
- 1 ½ cups low sodium chicken broth
- 2 tsp brown sugar
- 2 packets ramen noodles
- 4 cups coleslaw mix
- 1 cup matchstick carrots

Directions

1. Cook ground beef, add salt.
2. Add soy sauce, chicken broth, and brown sugar.
3. Bring to a strong simmer.
4. Add ramen noodles and cook. Flip ramen to evenly coat in sauce.
5. Stir in slaw and carrots.

Spaghetti Squash

Ingredients

- 2 spaghetti squash
- 1 lb ground turkey
- 1 package cherry tomatoes
- parmesan cheese
- 1 jar marinara sauce

Directions

1. Preheat oven to 400 F. Bake entire squash for 15 min. This will make it easier to cut.
2. When squash is finished baking, cut in half. Use a spoon to scrape out insides and seeds. (Just like a pumpkin!) Coat with olive oil, season with S+P and Italian seasoning.
3. Place cut squash in oven and bake for 30 min.
4. Over medium heat, cook ground turkey. Dice cherry tomatoes, and add to the cooked turkey. Smash tomatoes while cooking. Add marinara sauce.
5. When squash is done, use a fork to scrape the sides, creating spaghetti. Add toppings.

Ground Beef Bowl

• Makes 4 servings •

Ingredients

- 1 lb lean ground beef
- 2 cups rice
- 1 large bag frozen broccoli
- 2 cups chicken broth
- Mexican blend shredded cheese

Directions

1. Cook ground beef in a large skillet over medium heat. (Bonus tip: I like to add half a finely chopped onion and cook before adding beef, but this isn't necessary) Season ground beef as you like, I use chili powder and paprika.
2. Add broth, rice, and broccoli.
3. Stir mixture thoroughly, cover, and let simmer 10-15 minutes or until rice is cooked.
4. Turn heat off and remove pan from heat.
5. Top with cheese.

Tostadas

Ingredients

- tilapia- frozen fillets
- 1 container cherry tomatoes
- 1 package mini cucumbers
- 2 avocados
- 2-3 limes
- sour cream
- tostadas
- cilantro

Optional
- peppers
- onions

Directions

1. Dice tomatoes, cucumbers, and avocado. Finely chop cilantro. Mix ingredients together in a bowl.
2. Heat pan on medium heat and drizzle with oil. Cook tilapia. Tilapia does not take long to cook, about 2-3 min per side.
3. As tilapia cooks, begin using a spatula to break it up into small pieces. Continue until fish is fully cooked and evenly shredded.
4. Move tilapia to a large bowl, or keep in pan if there is room for all ingredients. Mix in tomatoes, cucumbers, avocado, and cilantro.
5. Cut limes in half and squeeze lime juice into mixture. Mix well. Add more lime juice to taste.
6. Spread sour cream on tostada and add fish mix.

Teriyaki Chicken & Fried Rice

Ingredients

- 2-3 chicken breasts
- 2 cups rice
- ¼ cup teriyaki sauce
- 2 tbsp soy sauce
- frozen mixed vegetables
- 3 eggs

Directions

1. Cut chicken into bite sized pieces. (To make this recipe even easier, buy pre-cut chicken.)
2. Heat oil in a large pan.
3. Add chicken, season with salt and pepper, and cook for 8-10 minutes.
4. Mix in teriyaki and soy sauce.
5. Mix in frozen vegetables and cook.
6. In a bowl, scramble 3 eggs. Pour into pan and cook, mixing with rice and veggies.
7. Add soy sauce to taste.

Sausage & White Bean Soup

Ingredients

- 1 package kielbasa sausage (12-14 oz)
- 3 cups chicken broth
- 2 cans white kidney beans
- 1 large bag spinach

Directions

1. Begin by heating a large saucepan over medium heat. Coat with oil. Slice sausage into even pieces. Place sausage into saucepan and cook for 10-15 minutes.
2. Add beans and chicken broth. Let simmer over medium heat for 5 minutes.
3. Add spinach. Stir and let cook until wilted.

SNACKS

Energy Bites

• Makes 24 bites •

Ingredients

- 2 cups oats
- 1 cup peanut butter
- 1 cup ground flaxseed
- 1 cup mini semisweet chocolate chips
- ⅓ cup honey
- 2 tsp vanilla extract

Directions

1. Mix all ingredients together in a large bowl.
2. Cover mixing bowl and chill in refrigerator 30 min-1 hour. This will help ingredients stick together.
3. Roll into bite-sized balls using a spoon and your hands. Store in fridge.

Notes

These are the perfect snack before an early morning lift or practice. It's important to have a little something to eat before any type of workout, and 1-2 of these bites are great when you don't feel like eating much.

Cinnamon Apple Dip

• Makes 1 serving •

Ingredients

- 1 apple for dipping
- ½ cup vanilla greek yogurt
- 1 tbsp peanut butter
- 1 tbsp pure maple syrup
- cinnamon

Directions

1. Mix yogurt, peanut butter, and maple syrup.
2. Sprinkle mixture with cinnamon.
3. Cut apple into slices and enjoy with the dip.

Veggies & Hummus

Ingredients

- veggies- whatever you like!
  - baby carrots
  - cucumbers
  - bell peppers
  - celery

- store-bought hummus

OR

- homemade-
- 1 can chickpeas
- drizzle of olive oil
- salt

Directions

1. Slice vegetables and place on plate.
2. For homemade hummus, mix 1 can chickpeas, drizzle of olive oil, and salt together in a blender. Mix until smooth. Add small amounts of water if the mixture is too thick. Enjoy with vegetables. Store leftovers in fridge.

Notes

When I am starving before dinner, throwing together a veggie tray is a quick and healthy way to snack. You can snack on it while you cook to prevent becoming too hangry. Also, try pairing hummus with pretzels!

Turkey & Cucumber Wrap

Ingredients

- turkey slices
- mini cucumbers
- hummus

Directions

1. Lay out turkey slice on a flat surface.
2. Spread hummus over turkey slice.
3. Cut ends off each cucumber. Slice cucumber lengthwise into 4 equal strips.
4. Place cucumber strip on one end of turkey slice and roll up to create wrap.

Peppers & Cottage Cheese

• Makes 1 serving •

Ingredients

- 1 bell pepper
- ½ cup cottage cheese
- everything bagel seasoning

Directions

1. Cut the bell pepper lengthwise into 4 equal sections, removing the stem, seeds, and white membranes from each piece to create "boats" for the filling.
2. Using a spoon, fill each slice with cottage cheese.
3. Sprinkle with everything bagel seasoning.

Greens Protein Shake

Ingredients

- 1 banana
- 1/2 cup frozen strawberries
- 1 cup spinach
- 1 scoop vanilla protein powder
- 1/2 cup milk
- handful of ice

Directions

Mix all ingredients in a blender until smooth.

Vanilla Protein Shake

Ingredients

- 1 cup milk or kefir
- 1 cup mixed frozen berries
- 2 tbsp peanut butter
- 1 scoop vanilla protein powder
- handful of ice

Directions

Mix all ingredients in a blender until smooth.

Chocolate Protein Shake

Ingredients

- 1 banana
- 1 scoop chocolate protein powder
- 1/2 cup milk
- 2 tbsp ground flaxseed
- 1 tbsp peanut butter
- 1 tbsp honey
- handful of ice

Directions

Mix all ingredients in a blender until smooth.

SWEET TREATS

Apple Crumble

Ingredients

- 1 apple
- ¼ cup oats
- cinnamon
- pure maple syrup

Directions

1. Saute 1 chopped apple in a pan until tender.
2. Sprinkle oats, cinnamon, and maple syrup on top of apple.
3. Let cook until golden and crisp, about 10-15 minutes.
4. Serve on top of Greek yogurt or ice cream.

Snickers Dates

Ingredients

- 16 medjool dates
- 1 cup dark chocolate chips
- nut butter of your choice
- 1 tbsp coconut oil

Directions

1. Line a cookie sheet with parchment paper.
2. Cut dates open and remove seed.
3. Use a spoon to fill date with nut butter. Pinch close.
4. Place dates in freezer to chill for 5 minutes.
5. In a bowl, add chocolate chips and coconut oil. You can use a spoonful of coconut oil, this will make the chocolate easier to melt.
6. Melt chocolate in microwave in 20-sec increments, stirring each time until smooth.
7. Using two forks to hold the date, dip and cover in the chocolate.
8. Place dates on cookie sheet and keep in the freezer for about 20 minutes or until hardened. Keep stored in refrigerator.

Chocolate Apple Dip

Ingredients

- ½ cup vanilla Greek yogurt
- 1 big scoop cocoa powder
- 1 tbsp peanut butter
- 1 tbsp honey
- mini chocolate chips
- apple

Directions

1. Start by mixing yogurt and cocoa powder in a bowl. Be careful with the cocoa powder- it can be messy.
2. Mix in peanut butter and honey until well combined and smooth.
3. Top with chocolate chips.
4. Cut apple into slices and use to dip into mixture.

Banana Bread Brownie

Ingredients

- 4-5 bananas
- ¼ cup cocoa powder
- 2 tbsp peanut butter
- 1 tbsp maple syrup
- 1 tsp vanilla
- 1 tsp baking soda
- chocolate chips

Directions

1. Preheat oven to 375 F.
2. Place bananas in a 8x8 inch baking dish and mash using a fork.
3. Add cocoa powder, peanut butter, maple syrup, vanilla, and baking soda. Mix until combined.
4. Add chocolate chips and mix.
5. Bake for 25-30 minutes.

Banana Bark

Ingredients

- 2 bananas
- peanut butter
- ½ cup chocolate chips

Directions

1. Slice bananas into thin pieces. Lay slices side by side on a plate.
2. Place banana slices in freezer for 15-20 minutes or until frozen.
3. Once frozen, spread peanut butter on banana slices.
4. In a separate cup or bowl, pour ½ cup chocolate chips. Melt in microwave in 20-second increments, stirring until smooth. This may take 3-4 times in the microwave.
5. Spread chocolate evenly on top of peanut butter.
6. Top with sea salt or chopped peanuts. Serve by cutting into equal squares.

Peach Turnover

• Makes 2 servings •

Ingredients

- 1 sliced peach
- 1 container crescent dough
- 3 tbsp maple syrup
- sprinkle of cinnamon

Directions

1. Slice peach into even, thin pieces. On a baking sheet, drizzle maple syrup in a small spot near the middle where you will place your turnover.
2. Evenly lie 5-6 pieces of the sliced peach on the maple syrup puddle so that they are in a straight row, overlapping each piece.
3. Drizzle peach slices with maple syrup and cinnamon.
4. Place a single square of puff pastry on top of the peaches, so that it covers all slices. Press down on pastry so that is sticks to the sheet pan.
5. Bake or air fry for 15 minutes at 350 F.
6. When finished baking, flip entire pastry over. Serve by itself or with ice cream!

About The Author

Abbey is a college softball player majoring in exercise science, with the goal of becoming a registered dietitian. She has a strong passion for fitness and nutrition and decided to create this cookbook after her teammates began asking her for recipes. When she's not in the kitchen or at the field, Abbey enjoys old music, plants, dark chocolate chips, playing guitar, being outside, Marvel movies, dogs, and spending time with family and friends.

You can follow Abbey on Instagram @activewabbs.